# Children's History of the World

# OXFORD
## Children's History of the World

# THE
# EARLY
# MODERN
# WORLD

Neil Grant

## OXFORD
UNIVERSITY PRESS

# OXFORD
## UNIVERSITY PRESS

Oxford University Press is a department of the University of Oxford.
It furthers the University's objective of excellence in research, scholarship,
and education by publishing worldwide in

Oxford  New York

Athens  Auckland  Bangkok  Bogotá  Buenos Aires  Kolkata
Cape Town  Chennai  Dar es Salaam  Delhi  Florence  Hong Kong  Istanbul
Karachi  Kuala Lumpur  Madrid  Melbourne  Mexico City  Mumbai
Nairobi  Paris  São Paulo  Shanghai  Singapore  Taipei  Tokyo  Toronto  Warsaw

with associated companies in  Berlin  Ibadan

Oxford is a registered trade mark of Oxford University Press
in the UK and in certain other countries

First published 2001
Some material in this book was previously
published in Children's History of the World 2000

British Library Cataloguing in Publication Data available

Paperback ISBN 0-19-910824-2

1 3 5 7 9 10 8 6 4 2

Printed in Malaysia

CONSULTANTS
Mike Corbishley
Dr. Narayani Gupta
Dr. Rick Halpern
Dr. Douglas H. Johnson
Rosemary Kelly
James Mason

# Contents

# How to use this book

*This book is divided into double-page spreads, each on a different subject. At the end of the book there is a Timeline. This shows at a glance the developments in different regions of the world during the period covered by the section. There is also a Who's Who page, which gives short biographies of the most important people of the period, a Glossary of important words, and an Index.*

The title describes the subject of the spread, like a newspaper headline.

The first paragraph sets the scene, explaining what the spread is about and why it is important.

The text is divided into short blocks, each with its own heading. They describe one part of the main subject of the spread.

Dates here show the time in history when the events took place.

---

## The Rise of Science

1500 - 1700

*People began to understand more about nature and the universe as a result of scientific discoveries in the 17th century. The invention of instruments such as the telescope and the microscope made these advances possible. Galileo's observations proved that the Earth moves around the Sun, and Newton explained why.*

### Science in the East

Before this time, science in China, India and Islamic countries was more advanced than in Europe. The Chinese were especially good at technology. More than 1,000 years ago they invented the abacus (the first calculator), clocks, rockets, paper and printing. They knew more about medicine than people in other countries.

The Hindus in India were ahead in mathematics. They invented the idea of 0 (zero) and the numbers we use today. In Islam, the caliphs of Baghdad encouraged science, as long as it did not contradict religious teaching. Arab astronomy and geography were the best in the world. The Arabs took their mathematics from the Hindus. They translated and studied the work of ancient Greek scholars, who had been forgotten in Europe.

▷ Scholars in this 16th-century observatory in Constantinople (Istanbul) are using instruments for taking measurements of the stars. At the back are a cross-staff, a quadrant and an astrolabe, all used by travellers to work out where they were from the position of the stars. The study of the stars was important in Islam. It helped the Muslims to work out the direction of Mecca from wherever they were, so they knew in which direction to pray.

▷ When Galileo heard how a Dutchman had invented the telescope in 1608, he immediately made one himself. With it he saw that the surface of the Moon was rough and uneven.

**Sensational discoveries**

1608 First telescope made by Lippershey.
1628 Harvey shows how blood circulates.
1658 Huygens makes pendulum clock.
1662 First study of statistics.
1673 Leeuwenhoek's microscope can magnify 200 times.
1676 Römer calculates speed of light.
1687 Newton publishes his theory of gravity.

### Learning about the universe

Before the 17th century, science was held back by the Christian Church, which punished anyone whose ideas disagreed with its teaching. Copernicus, a Polish monk, wrote a book on astronomy which denied the Church's belief that the Earth was the centre of the universe. He dared not publish it until he was dying, in 1543. Nearly 100 years later, an Italian called Galileo got into trouble for teaching Copernicus's ideas. He knew Copernicus was right because he had looked at the sky using a telescope. He saw that Jupiter has moons that move around it, just as our Moon moves around the Earth. Changes in the appearance of the planets showed that they were circling the Sun. Galileo's telescope solved many mysteries. He showed that the planets seem larger than the stars because they are nearer, and that the Milky Way is not just a sheet of light, but billions of separate stars.

However, Galileo could not explain why some planets move around others. It was an English scientist, Isaac Newton, who discovered the law of gravity which he explained in a book, known as Newton's *Principia* ('principles'), one of the greatest science books ever written. Newton saw that the orbit of the Moon depends on the same force that makes an apple fall to Earth – the force of gravity.

△ When Robert Hooke made his microscope he was able to see a tiny flea clearly enough to make this detailed drawing.

### Studying living things

The most sensational discoveries of the Scientific Revolution were in mathematics, physics and astronomy, but people also made important advances in other sciences, especially biology. A book on the human body by a Flemish doctor called Vesalius (1543) described the organs of the body, with brilliant drawings based on his dissections. This helped William Harvey, an Englishman, to understand how the blood circulates through the body (1628). Many discoveries followed Leeuwenhoek's invention of a better microscope. Robert Hooke, an Englishman, was the first to describe the cells of living things.

**Scientific societies**

*Universities began to take science seriously. Gresham College, London (1575) had lectures in astronomy. Sir Isaac Newton (right) studied mathematics and science at Cambridge University, England. From 1660 scientific societies or clubs, like the English Royal Society and the French Academy of Science, were founded. By bringing scientists together to discuss their ideas, they encouraged scientific progress.*

29

---

Fact boxes list key events associated with the subject.

Photographs and illustrations show paintings, objects, places, people and scenes from the past.

Coloured boxes give more details about major events or important people linked to the subject.

Captions describe the illustrations and how they relate to the main text.

Many pages also have a map, to show the country or region where the events took place.

# Introduction

*Before 1500 the world's main centres of civilisation were divided from each other, and a kind of balance existed between them. But between 1500 and 1800 that balance began to break down. The process began with the changes in Europe which together are known as the Renaissance and the Reformation. They introduced a new age, in which life changed at a faster and faster rate, driven by new ideas, new activities and new institutions.*

Among these new institutions was the nation-state, ruled by a powerful monarch, and eager to increase its power and wealth. Strong rivalry existed between them, with first Spain and later France, as the most powerful.

For the rest of the world, the most important development in Renaissance Europe was the discovery of the seas. Sailors like Columbus made the oceans of the world into Europe's transport system. The two continents of North and South America, which had been unknown to people from other continents, were drawn into the world by European settlers. For the American peoples, the result was disaster. Their old way of life was almost completely destroyed. They became workers, servants, slaves. The disaster spread to Africa, where Europeans bought slaves to work in their colonies.

European ships appeared in the ports of Asia. They were not welcome, because they seized much of the sea-borne trade. European merchants and missionaries visited other countries, but they had little effect on the civilisations of Asia, which were older than their own. In war, great powers like the Ottoman Turks were more than a match for European armies. In fact the Turks captured much of south-east Europe. The Mughal emperor of India treated European visitors kindly, but kept them at at a safe distance. The Chinese simply ignored them, and the Japanese threw them out.

Yet by the 1780s, Europeans were established all over the world. A few Europeans had visited Australia, another country that had been almost cut off from the rest of the world. In the Americas, the European colonies had grown so fast that they would soon become independent nations themselves. And meanwhile, in spite of fighting so many wars among themselves, the Europeans had become much richer and more powerful. New powers appeared, such as Russia, whose empire included 12 million square kilometres of Asia. European science and technology had raced ahead of other continents, but so far it had little effect on the lives of ordinary people. That would soon change too.

# Voyages of Exploration

*In the 15th century, European sailors began to explore the oceans looking for new trade routes. By 1550 they had sailed around the world, visited every continent except Antarctica, and set up trading posts and colonies in Asia, Africa and the Americas.*

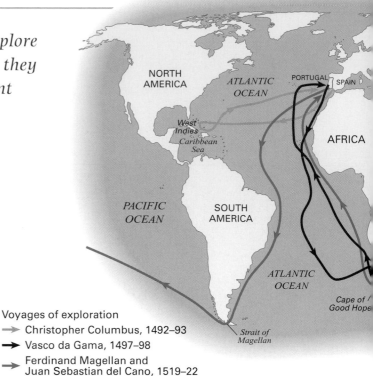

## Trade routes

Since ancient times, Europeans had imported luxury goods, such as silk and spices, from Asia. These goods passed through many hands to get to Europe, and were always expensive. The rise of the Ottoman Empire had closed many overland trade routes, so the Europeans wanted to find a route to the East by sea. No one knew if there was one. Ships had never sailed far from land. Many people still believed the Earth was flat, and thought ships could sail off the edge. Even people who knew that the Earth was round believed that it was much smaller than it is. No one had any idea that the Americas existed, so it was a complete surprise to Europeans when this 'new world' was found by explorers looking for new ways to the East.

Voyages of exploration
→ Christopher Columbus, 1492–93
→ Vasco da Gama, 1497–98
→ Ferdinand Magellan and
  Juan Sebastian del Cano, 1519–22

### European voyages

1488 Dias passes the Cape of Good Hope, South Africa.
1492 Columbus crosses the Atlantic.
1497 Cabot sails from England to Newfoundland.
1498 Vasco da Gama finds the route to India via East Africa.
1534 Cartier enters the St Lawrence River, Canada

△ The best route to India and the Far East was followed by Vasco da Gama. The western route was blocked by Columbus's 'New World'. Later captains, still believing that Asia lay close by, tried to find a way past or through it. In 1519 Ferdinand Magellan sailed around South America and became the first European to cross the Pacific Ocean. One of his ships reached home in 1522, having sailed around the world. But this route to the East was too long and dangerous to be useful.

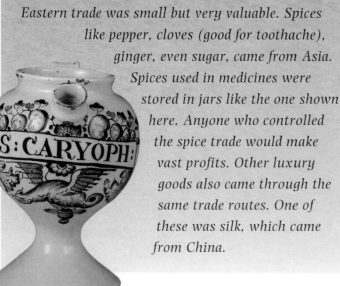

### The spice trade

*Eastern trade was small but very valuable. Spices like pepper, cloves (good for toothache), ginger, even sugar, came from Asia. Spices used in medicines were stored in jars like the one shown here. Anyone who controlled the spice trade would make vast profits. Other luxury goods also came through the same trade routes. One of these was silk, which came from China.*

## The Portuguese

The first explorers of the oceans were the Portuguese. Portuguese sea captains explored the West African coast, hoping to find the source of African gold and a route to the East. In 1487 Bartolomeu Dias reached the south-western tip of Africa, the Cape, opening the way to the Indian Ocean. Ten years later Vasco da Gama followed with a large, well-armed fleet. He visited the trading cities of East Africa, and from one of them, Malindi, an Arab pilot guided him across the Indian Ocean. A sea route from Europe to Asia had been found! In a few years, he and other Portuguese captains seized the Indian Ocean trade from Indian and Arab merchants. They pressed on to the spice islands of the Pacific.

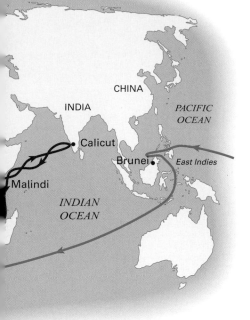

▷ Columbus and his crew of 40 men sailed in the *Santa Maria*, a tough merchant ship about 30 m long. She was later wrecked in the West Indies, but Columbus also had two smaller ships. At sea, Columbus could work out his latitude (his position between north and south), but he had to rely on good guesswork for his longitude (his position between east and west).

## Columbus

Christopher Columbus, an Italian captain, hoped to find a route to the East by sailing west. After other governments had turned him down, he got support from Spain. In 1492 he landed in the Caribbean. He believed he was on the edge of Asia, and called the islands he found the Indies, thinking they were the East Indies. They were later called the West Indies.

Spain set up colonies in the West Indies and began to explore the mainland. Hundreds of adventurous Spaniards arrived. Most hoped to find gold and make a fortune, but some were Christian missionaries who wanted to convert the local people. In 1499 another Italian captain working for Spain, Amerigo Vespucci, discovered the Amazon River. The new continent of America was named after him.

▷ The native peoples of the Americas had never seen guns, horses, or large ships. These Aztecs are fighting the Spaniards. On the left one of them wears a jaguar skin.

## Other nations

The Pope declared that the world should be divided between Spain and Portugal. A vertical line was drawn through a map of the Atlantic. Spain had the Americas to the West, Portugal had Brazil and the East Indies. Other Europeans did not accept this. In 1497 John Cabot, an Italian captain working for England, reached Newfoundland. Between 1534 and 1536 a Frenchman, Jacques Cartier, discovered the St Lawrence River and reached what is now Montreal. Later, Cabot's and Cartier's voyages led to the setting up of English colonies in Massachusetts and Virginia, and French colonies in Canada.

# The European Renaissance

*In Europe by the 15th and 16th centuries people were becoming much more curious about the world around them. This was one reason for the voyages of exploration. People also developed new ideas about art, science and religion which led to big changes in Europe.*

## A rebirth of learning

Renaissance means 'rebirth'. It was a rebirth of interest in the art and learning of ancient Greece and Rome, which reached its peak in Italy at this time. For centuries, the Church had been the centre of learning and art, and the Classical civilisations had been mostly forgotten. Now scholars made new translations of the work of ancient writers. They discovered that these people, who had lived over 1,000 years earlier, often understood the world better than they did. This interest in ancient learning inspired humanist scholars to think for themselves, and led them on to great discoveries in art and learning. The scholars are called humanists because they were interested in people and in the world around them. It was a very exciting time, and people felt there was no limit to what they could discover or do.

▽ The cathedral of Florence, in Italy. This magnificent building was finished about 1436, and many famous Renaissance artists worked on it. The dome on the cathedral was designed by Filippo Brunelleschi, and was the first large dome built in Europe since the 6th century.

## The spread of the Renaissance

The Renaissance flourished in different parts of Europe at different times. It reached its peak in northern Italy, the most advanced region in Europe. Wealthy merchants and princes of the city states, such as the popes in Rome or the Medici family of Florence, spent their money on beautiful buildings and works of art. They encouraged the best artists to make things for them.

Renaissance ideas spread all over Europe. In the Netherlands rich merchants also wanted paintings. Artists here developed the technique of oil painting. The most famous humanist scholar in Europe was a Dutchman called Erasmus.

△ Michelangelo painting the ceiling of the Pope's Chapel in Rome, with scenes from the Bible. One of the greatest geniuses of the Renaissance, Michelangelo was a sculptor, painter, architect (he designed most of St Peter's Basilica in Rome) and poet. The chapel's ceiling is larger than a basketball court, and it took Michelangelo over four years to paint it.

## *Printed books*

*The most important invention of the Renaissance was printing with metal type. This picture shows a Renaissance printer's workshop. The first metal type was used by Johannes Gutenberg, in Germany in the 1450s. Before that, books were written by hand or printed with wood blocks. Now they could be printed in many copies, more cheaply and quickly. New ideas could spread faster. Although scholars still wrote in Latin, some writers used their own language.*

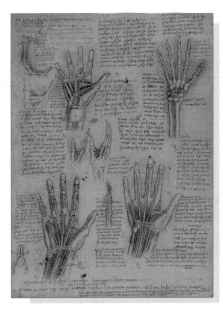

△ Leonardo's notebooks are full of drawings of marvellous machines, and studies of the human body, like this one. He wrote his notes in back-to-front writing.

## Science

As people were interested in all kinds of knowledge, scholars would study many different subjects, not specialise in one area. Leonardo da Vinci, an Italian, was an example of 'Renaissance man'. He is remembered best as a painter, but he was also a military expert, engineer, and inventor. He dissected dead bodies to understand how bones and muscles work.

## Literature

As in painting and sculpture, the subjects of literature became more realistic, and less based on religious stories. Plays were performed in specially built theatres, instead of in the street or in the courtyards of inns. These were the first permanent theatres since the time of the Romans. The plays of the English Renaissance writer William Shakespeare (1564–1616) were written to be performed in these theatres.

▷ William Shakespeare

# The Reformation

*For over 1,000 years there was one Christian Church in western Europe. It was ruled by the Pope in Rome. In the 16th century, some people, and some states, broke away from the Church, and Christians divided into Roman Catholics and Protestants.*

## Complaints about the Church

Some Christians in the 16th century complained that all sorts of churchmen, from the Pope down to ordinary priests and monks, did not behave like Christians. The Pope ruled a large part of Italy, and he seemed more interested in power and wealth than in God. Bishops were often harsh landlords. Many priests were ignorant, lazy and dishonest. People began to protest about the way the Church was run, so they became known as Protestants. Although at first they wanted to stay in the Roman Catholic Church and improve it, in the end they formed their own new churches.

## Martin Luther

Martin Luther (1483-1546), a German priest, was the first great reformer. He criticised the Pope for taking money from people in return for forgiving their sins. Luther believed that only God could forgive sinners. The Pope expelled Luther from the Church because of his criticisms. But Luther had many followers, including some German princes. These Lutherans left the Roman Catholic Church.

The Reformation spread. The reformers complained that church services and the Bible were both in Latin, the language of ancient Rome, which ordinary people could not understand. They thought the Church was keeping people ignorant so it could control them. Luther translated some of the Bible into German.

▽ In 1517 Luther fastened 95 complaints about the Church on the church door (often used as a notice board) in Wittenberg, Germany. That act marks the beginning of the Reformation.

◁ John Calvin was a reformer who led the Protestants in Geneva, Switzerland. He taught that only those specially chosen by God, the 'elect', would go to heaven when they died. The 'elect' were Calvin's followers. Calvin's ideas spread even more widely than Luther's, especially in the Netherlands and Scotland.

### The destruction of English monasteries

*Some rulers gained power and wealth by rejecting the Roman Catholic Church and the Pope. When Henry VIII of England made himself head of a national Church, he increased his royal power. He closed down the monasteries, and took over their lands, which greatly increased his income. In the process, many pieces of religious art were destroyed.*

## The Counter-Reformation

After the Reformation, the Roman Catholic Church did reform itself. Strong popes demanded better behaviour from churchmen. A new religious order was founded, the Society of Jesus. Its members, called Jesuits, started schools and became missionaries to convert people to Roman Catholicism.

## Religious wars

The divisions between Catholics and Protestants brought wars and persecution. In most countries the Church and government were closely linked. Rulers did not want their people to practise different forms of religion. They were afraid that if people did not obey the Church, they might decide not to obey the government either.

In France, where the king was a Catholic, there were civil wars between Catholics and Protestants (called Huguenots). These ended when the Huguenot leader became King Henri IV. He had to become a Catholic, but he gave the Huguenots freedom to worship as they wanted, in the Edict of Nantes, in 1598. Protestants in the northern Netherlands rebelled against their Spanish, Catholic rulers.

The Netherlands became independent from Spain in 1609.

The Thirty Years' War (1618-48) began as a war between Protestant German princes and the Catholic Holy Roman Emperor. It turned into a struggle for power between different European countries, with the powerful Catholic countries, Spain and France, fighting on opposite sides.

△ The Massacre of St Bartholomew's Eve. On 24 August 1572 the French king planned to assassinate leaders of the Huguenots in Paris. Things got out of hand, and tens of thousands of ordinary Huguenots were killed.

# Spanish and Portuguese Empires

*In the 16th century, Europeans spread their power around the world. The leaders were Spain and Portugal. Portugal gained control of the valuable spice trade. At the same time Spain founded an empire in the Americas and became rich from the silver discovered there.*

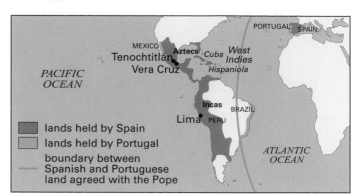

## The Portuguese Empire

Once the Portuguese had gained control of the Indian Ocean, they moved farther east. They wanted to control trade with the Moluccas, known as the 'Spice Islands'. Their greatest empire-builder was Albuquerque. He built a large base at Goa in west India, and in 1511 he captured the important Malayan port of Malacca. In 1512 the Portuguese reached the 'Spice Islands', and in 1513 Albuquerque captured Ormuz, in south Persia. This gave the Portuguese control of the Persian Gulf. By 1556, the Portuguese had a base at Macao, China. To the west, Portugal claimed Brazil in the Americas. Portugal's main interest was in controlling trade – it did not want to colonise these new lands it claimed.

△ The line dividing the non-Christian world between Portugal and Spain was fixed in 1494.

▽ The battle for Tenochtitlán. The Aztec city was on an island in a lake, joined to the mainland by a causeway. The Spaniards destroyed the city and built what is now Mexico City.

CONQVISTA DE MEXICO POR CORTES. N.7

## The Spanish Americas

Except for Brazil, the Americas 'belonged' to Spain. The Spanish conquests were organised by adventurers who hoped to make their fortune. Cortés, an official in Cuba, heard stories of a wealthy state deep inland. With 500 men he landed at Vera Cruz, Mexico, in 1517. The local people were willing to help him against the Aztecs who ruled them. Montezuma, the Aztec emperor, allowed the Spaniards into the city of Tenochtitlán, but trouble soon broke out. With the help of the other local people, the Spaniards captured Tenochtitlán, and the Aztec empire fell into Spanish hands. Cortés became ruler of what was called 'New Spain', an area larger than Spain itself.

The other great American empire was the Inca Empire in Peru. It was already weakened by a civil war, so it was conquered even more easily. Francisco Pizarro arrived in 1531 with only 180 men. The Inca ruler, Atahualpa, let them in, but they ambushed him and captured the capital, Quito. In the next few years Pizarro's followers took over the whole Inca Empire.

△ The Inca made wonderful objects of gold, like this llama. Atahualpa promised the Spaniards a hoard of gold if they would let him go. The Spanish took the treasure, but killed Atahualpa as well.

## The Spanish Empire

The Spanish explored 'New Spain' looking for 'El Dorado', a legendary city of gold. During their search they killed many American people, but they never found the city. They did, however, find silver mines in Mexico and Peru. Every year, they sent home large fleets of ships loaded with silver. Spain became for a time the richest and most powerful country in Europe.

Spanish people were given large estates in America, and made the native Americans their slaves. Although the Spanish government and Christian missionaries tried to give the slaves some protection, many died from overwork and cruel treatment. Even more died of European diseases. To replace the native Americans, new slaves were brought from Africa.

△ At first, European traders bought furs from native hunters. Later, a new kind of hunter developed, the 'runners of the woods', part French, and part American.

## New England and New France

Other European nations refused to accept the division of the world between Portugal and Spain. However, the English, French and Dutch did not settle in colonies in the Americas until over 100 years later. By then, Spanish power was weakening.

The French started settlements in 'New France' (south-east Canada) to exploit the valuable fur trade, but not many people settled there permanently. In 1682 a French explorer, La Salle, travelled from the Great Lakes, along the Mississippi to the Gulf of Mexico. He claimed the region for France. This threatened the English colonies, and England and France fought over land in North America until the French were defeated in 1763.

Some of the most profitable American colonies proved be the rich, sugar-growing Caribbean islands.

# European Nations

*In the 16th century, Europe was becoming a group of independent nations. Most were ruled by powerful kings. Their people began to feel they belonged to one nation, and that it was their duty to be loyal to their monarch.*

## 'New monarchies'

In the 16th century rulers had more control than in earlier times. Kings chose their own ministers, who ran the country instead of powerful lords. The kings had royal courts to provide justice, and some had professional armies to control the country and fight foreigners. But kings also needed the support of their people. To get this they had to keep the country orderly and the people prosperous. They were helped by the fact that the population was growing, and so were trade and business. Kings supported business with special privileges.

In 1400 there was no single great power in Europe. The French king controlled only a third of France, because the king of England and the Duke of Burgundy owned large parts of the country. But by 1453 the English had been driven out, and in 1477 Burgundy was divided up and France took half of it. France became a strong and united kingdom. The same happened in other parts of Europe. In Russia, the Grand Duke of Muscovy became tsar of Russia, and in Sweden the strong Vasa kings made their country independent from Denmark.

△ The marriage of Ferdinand of Aragon and Isabella of Castille, in 1479, joined the two main Spanish kingdoms. When the last Muslim kingdom was defeated in 1492, Spain was united for the first time.

### The powerful Tudors

*In the 15th century there was a long civil war in England over who should be king. The first Tudor king, Henry VII, won his crown in battle in 1485, and worked hard to make his throne secure. His son Henry VIII (above) increased his power when he made himself Supreme Head of the Church of England in 1534. Henry VIII's daughter, Elizabeth I, coped skilfully with dangers at home and abroad, even though people then did not believe a woman could rule successfully. English sailors such as Francis Drake challenged Spanish power in the New World, and managed to defeat the great Spanish fleet, the Armada, which tried to invade England in 1588.*

▽ The house of a rich English wool merchant in the 16th century. The wool trade was still the biggest business in Europe.

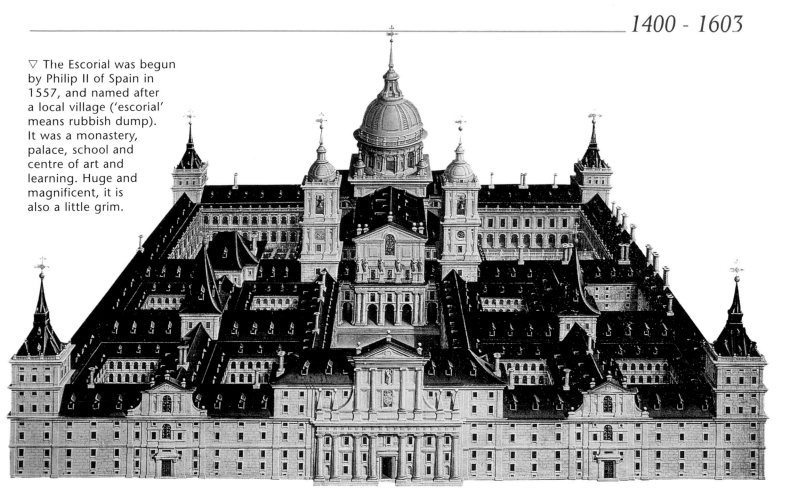

▽ The Escorial was begun by Philip II of Spain in 1557, and named after a local village ('escorial' means rubbish dump). It was a monastery, palace, school and centre of art and learning. Huge and magnificent, it is also a little grim.

## Germany and Italy

Not all monarchs were as successful as the Tudors. The kings of Poland and Hungary built empires in the 15th century, but they did not last long, because the Ottoman Turks conquered south-east Europe and threatened Germany. The King of the Germans was the Holy Roman Emperor, but he could not control the German princes, who ruled as independent monarchs. One of the emperor's difficulties was that he had too many responsibilities. Charles V (emperor 1519-58) ruled over Italy, which was divided into several different states, as well as Germany and the Netherlands. He also ruled Spain and the Spanish possessions in America. This huge empire could not be run by one government. When Charles gave up his thrones, the empire went to his brother, and the Spanish crown to his son.

## Spain

Under Charles's son Philip II, Spain was the greatest kingdom in Europe, thanks to its wealth from American silver. This wealth and power made them enemies, especially after Spain took over Portugal (1580). English and French ships attacked their empire. American silver drove up prices, and made Spaniards believe they need not work for a living, causing the country's decline in the 17th century.

### The rise of bankers

Banks hardly existed before the 14th century, because the Church taught that lending money and charging interest was a sin. Banking started with merchant-bankers like the Medici in Italy, who bought and sold goods on credit. Banking was usually a family business, and some families became very rich. The most famous German bankers were the Fuggers of Augsburg, who made a fortune by lending money to the Emperor Charles V. But lending money to great monarchs was risky. They did not always pay it back.

# The Persian Empire

*The Safavid Empire of Persia (modern Iran) was the smallest of the three Islamic empires. It did not last long, but its arts were brilliant, and its influence has lasted to the present.*

△ The Safavid Empire depended on a great leader, Abbas I, who united it and made it strong. It lasted over 100 years, but the Ottoman Empire lasted much longer.

Safavid Persian Empire in 1628
Ottoman Empire in 1683

## The divisions of Islam

In the 15th century, Islam covered a larger region than Christianity. It was divided into many groups, or sects. In the early 16th century, at about the same time as the Reformation in Europe, Islam went through a time of crisis. This was caused partly by the rise of the Safavids. They were Shi'ite Muslims from Azerbaijan, named after their founder, a Sufi named Safi al-Din. They became the greatest power in Persia, and in 1502 their leader, Ismail, made himself shah. Many years passed, and many battles were fought, before Ismail controlled the whole of Persia.

## Ismail I

Under Ismail, the Safavid Empire grew to an area larger than modern Iran. It included Persians, Turkmen, Arabs and other peoples. Ismail made his form of Shi'ism the religion of Persia (as it still is today). His followers believed he should be the head of all Islam. That was a threat to other Muslim rulers, especially the Ottoman sultan. The Ottoman Turks and the Persians were already quarrelling over land, so fighting became inevitable. When the Ottomans invaded, Ismail could not stop them seizing his land and killing thousands of people. People said that after this defeat, Ismail never smiled again. The fighting between the Safavids and the Ottomans continued for over 100 years.

△ A caravanserai was a kind of travellers' inn. It provided food and shelter for merchants' caravans. Shah Abbas made his people build good roads, bridges, and caravanseries, to assist trade.

## Abbas the Great

The Safavid Empire was at its height during the rule of Shah Abbas (1586-1628). He created an army of trained soldiers, which drove out the invading Uzbeks, regained all the territory taken by the Ottomans, and captured Baghdad. These victories helped him to unite the peoples of Persia into one nation. Abbas was more tolerant than earlier rulers. He even allowed Christian missionaries into his empire. Europeans brought trade, but he was annoyed by the Portuguese, who controlled trade in the Persian Gulf. He recaptured Ormuz from them in 1622. Abbas is remembered for his skill in government and his encouragement of trade, industry and the arts. He ruthlessly protected his own power, but he created a rich and powerful country.

▽ Shah Abbas built a new capital at Isfahan, one of the world's most beautiful cities. It was a place of glittering mosques and minarets, pavilions, orchards, streams, and lively bazaars.

### Carpets

*People in many Asian countries made rugs and carpets, knotted by hand. Persian carpets, filled with flowers and animals, are perhaps the most beautiful.*

## Nadir Shah

Later Safavid rulers did not have Abbas's skill or intelligence. They wasted their time in plots and feuds. The empire was conquered by the Afghans in 1722, but in 1736 the throne was seized by Nadir Shah. He had been leader of a large band of robbers, but was a brilliant military leader. Nadir Shah was the last of the great Asian conquerors. He drove out Afghans, Turks, and others, and created an empire larger than the Safavids', conquering northern India. But he had no other skills. He was cruel and greedy, and in the end he was killed by his own soldiers.

# The Ottoman Empire

*The Ottoman Turkish Empire was the greatest power in the world in the early 16th century. It included parts of three continents: Asia, Africa and Europe. For most Muslims, the Ottoman sultan was the leader of all Islam.*

## The rise of the Ottomans

When the earlier empire of the Seljuk Turks was attacked by the Mongols (1243), the Ottomans took over. During the 14th century they rapidly gained land, mostly taken from the Byzantine Empire. In 1453 the Ottomans captured Constantinople. This, finally, marked the end of the 1,100 year-old Byzantine Empire. Under Selim the Grim (1512-20) the Ottomans added Egypt, Syria and part of Safavid Persia to their empire.

◁ The key to Ottoman success was the world's first professional army, the Janissaries. They were mostly Christians from peasant families, who were taken to Constantinople when they were boys and educated to be Muslim soldiers. They lived by their own rules in their own barracks. They were very loyal to the sultan, who gave them special privileges. In later times, however, their strength and independence made them a threat to weaker rulers.

▽ To win more land in south-east Europe, the Turks had to take Constantinople. They finally captured it in 1453, with the aid of a giant cannon (it was not really much use as it could only fire once every few hours).

## Suleiman the Magnificent

Ottoman power and wealth was greatest under Suleiman I (1520-66). Europeans called him 'the Magnificent', because they were impressed by his splendid court. Suleiman's subjects called him 'the Lawgiver', because he was a good governor. The Ottoman Empire under Suleiman was prosperous as well as powerful. It had a large population and plenty of rich farm land. There were good hospitals and schools, and little crime. Although Suleiman was a Muslim, he accepted people of other religions. He employed Greek-speaking Christians from the old Byzantine Empire, and appointed Christian governors in the newly conquered Balkans (south-east Europe). Suleiman was also a good war leader. His armies captured Aden and Algiers, and took the fortress of the Knights of St John on the island of Rhodes. In 1525 they won Hungary. They even threatened the heart of Europe, by besieging Vienna in 1529.

### The Ottoman navy

*One weakness of all the great Muslim empires was that they had no navy to match their armies. Suleiman found a man to create one: Kheir-ed-din, called 'Barbarossa' ('red beard') by Europeans. He was a North African captain, famous for his raids against Christian ships and towns in the Mediterranean. With Suleiman's support, he built a powerful navy of war galleys, which gave the Sultan command of the eastern Mediterranean.*

▷ Suleimaniyeh, the Mosque of Suleiman in Istanbul. Suleiman employed the great architect Sinan to build mosques, palaces, schools and hospitals throughout the empire. The mosque still stands today, a reminder of the golden age of the Ottoman Empire.

## The decline of the Ottomans

Many of the sultans who came after Suleiman were poor leaders. They concentrated on quarrels within their large court, instead of on government, trade and industry. The population kept growing, but the empire's wealth did not. In 1571 a combined Christian fleet defeated the Ottoman navy at the battle of Lepanto, so the Ottomans lost control of the Mediterranean. The empire sometimes became powerful again under good rulers. In fact it was at its largest in the late 17th century, when the able Kuprili family served as chief ministers and the Ottoman armies again besieged Vienna (1683). But the empire could not keep that strength. The Ottomans lost most of their lands in Europe and Africa in the 19th century, and the last sultan was finally deposed when the modern Turkish Republic was founded in 1922.

# Mughal India

*The third great Muslim empire of the 16th century was the empire of the Mughals. They united most of India and ruled for more than 200 years.*

## Akbar

'Mughal' comes from the name 'Mongol'. Babur ('Tiger'), who was the first of the Mughal emperors, was a descendant of the Mongol conqueror, Tamerlane. Babur conquered Afghanistan and began the conquest of India in 1525. His grandson, Akbar (1556-1605), was only 17 when he took command. He conquered the whole of northern India. Although the Mughals won their empire by force, Akbar kept it by good government.

▷ The Rajputs were the fiercest opponents of the Mughal conquerors. They were a caste of warriors from north-west India, famous for their bravery and independence. Akbar won their support by a mixture of force and friendship. One of his wives was a Rajput princess.

Muslim rule was not new in northern India, but Akbar won over Hindus by showing them respect. He married a Hindu princess, attended Hindu festivals and employed Hindu officials as well as Muslims. He brought peace and justice to places that had not seen them before.

It is said that Akbar could not read. But he certainly had a vast amount read to him, and during his reign Mughal style and customs fascinated all Indians, as well as foreigners.

### Akbar's palace

*Akbar built the magnificent ceremonial centre of Fatehpur-Sikri, near his capital, Agra, because it was the birthplace of his son and successor, Jahangir. There he listened to the arguments of Muslims, Hindus, Jesuits and others. He once suggested that a Christian with a Bible and a Muslim with the Koran should step into the fire to see who was burned. They politely refused.*

▽ Although the Mughal Empire was largest under Aurangzeb, it was less peaceful, as the Mughal government was breaking down.

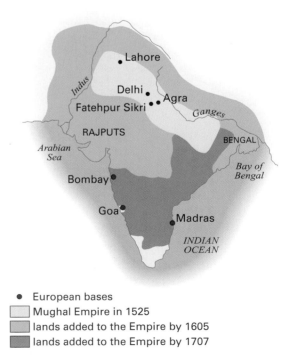

- ● European bases
- Mughal Empire in 1525
- lands added to the Empire by 1605
- lands added to the Empire by 1707

## Shah Jahan

Mughal rule after Akbar was more strict. Shah Jahan (1628-53) even ordered Hindu temples to be destroyed, although his order was not obeyed. In the 18th century, Europeans were able to control the seas and parts of the coast because the Mughals did not have a navy. The Mughal Empire continued to grow, but it was no longer so rich. Taxes were so high that peasants left their land, to avoid paying them. The roads, which Akbar's good government had made safe, became the hunting ground of bandits.

▽ The Taj Mahal, the most famous of the many marvellous buildings of the Mughals. It is a tomb built by Shah Jahan for his favourite wife. He is buried there too.

## Aurangzeb

Under Aurangzeb (1658-1707) the empire was at its largest. But the costs were high. Aurangzeb was often away fighting, so the country was not governed properly, and rebellions increased. After his death, the Mughal emperors steadily lost their power. In 1738 Nadir Shah captured Delhi and carried off the treasures of the Mughal court. With no strong central government left, the Europeans gradually moved in. By 1765 the greatest power in India was not the Mughal emperor, but the British East India Company. This was a trading company, but in order to increase its own trade and profits it became a ruling power. It took over Bengal in 1757, and by 1815 it controlled most of India, either directly through a governor, or by dominating the local Indian princes.

# The Expansion of China

*Life in China changed very little over the centuries. In spite of rebellions, civil wars and foreign rule, Chinese civilisation was preserved by a small group of learned men, called mandarins, who ran everyday government.*

## The Ming dynasty

The Ming took over from the Mongols of the Yuan dynasty in 1368. Under the strong rule of the early Ming emperors, the Chinese Empire was restored to health. Farming improved, thanks to new crops, canals and irrigation works. The Ming even tried to help the hard-worked peasants, against the big landowners. In the towns, industry flourished, especially cloth-making. In the city of Nanking, there were about 50,000 looms for weaving silk. European traders paid in silver for Chinese tea, silk and porcelain, so Chinese merchants grew rich. The population was growing again.

◁ The Chinese potters under the Ming and Manchu were magnificent artist-craftsmen. This vase was made during the late Ming period. Europeans were astonished by these imported pots, which they called 'china'.

△ The Manchu emperors conquered Mongolia and Tibet, and pushed the Chinese Empire into central Asia.

Ming China, 1368
Manchu China at its largest, about 1760
Manchu homeland
--- Great Wall

▷ Mandarins were imperial officials. The colour of the knob on a mandarin's hat showed his rank. Mandarins were also scholars, artists and landowners. They had to pass an exam to become officials.

## The end of the Ming

With rising industry and trade, a rich middle class began to develop. But the landowners and upper-class officials still held all the power. They jealously guarded their position against rivals. At the same time, the Ming emperors were losing their early energy. Although they ordered the Great Wall to be rebuilt, it did not prevent raids by the Mongols. Japanese pirates attacked the coast and sailed up the Yangtze River to raid inland cities. The Ming were losing control. After 1582, they left government to greedy and dishonest palace officials. Rebellions broke out among the peasants and in towns. The Manchu, a warlike people from Manchuria, were asked to help restore order. Instead, they set up their own dynasty, the Qing, in 1644.

▷ The Forbidden City, built by the Ming as a home for the emperor and his family. It is a little city inside Beijing, the Ming capital. No one except royalty and officials could enter, on pain of death.

## The Qing dynasty

The Manchu emperors of the Qing dynasty did not try to change Chinese customs, though they did make officials wear pigtails (a Manchu custom) as a sign of loyalty. With peace and strong government, the Chinese grew richer. Intelligent Qing emperors encouraged art and learning. Under Kangxi (reigned 1661-1722) great works of literature were produced, including an encyclopedia of about 2,000 volumes.

Chinese civilisation seemed as strong and brilliant as ever. But it was not changing much. Although trade brought China into contact with Europe, which was changing fast, China stood still. By about 1800 the Qing, like the Ming before them, had lost control. Half the country was in revolt against the government. The navy could not leave port for fear of pirates. Europeans controlled Chinese trade. The old empire was doomed, yet somehow it lasted until 1911.

### Expeditions overseas

*From 1405 to 1433 Admiral Zheng Ho led great expeditions overseas, sailing as far as East Africa. His 60 ships, called junks, were larger and safer than European ships. He sailed to buy luxuries for the imperial court, and to collect taxes from Chinese colonies. Later, foreign voyages were forbidden, and any merchant caught trading abroad was executed.*

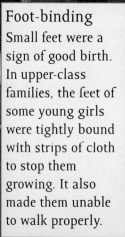

### Foot-binding

Small feet were a sign of good birth. In upper-class families, the feet of some young girls were tightly bound with strips of cloth to stop them growing. It also made them unable to walk properly.

# Tokugawa Japan

*From 1615 to 1854, Japan's rulers kept their country apart from the world. Foreigners were not allowed in, and Japanese were not allowed out. But after 1854, Japan began to change fast, and by 1900 it was the greatest power in Asia.*

## Shutting out the world

Under the rule of the Tokugawa shoguns, Japan was shut off from the world. The only foreigners allowed in were a few Dutch merchants, and they were only allowed on one small island. The Japanese needed them to supply Western products, especially guns. The shoguns did not allow the daimyo, the local lords, to have much power, and they also stopped raids by warriors on foreign coasts and ships. They wanted peace and order. People were supposed to follow the old customs, and stay in the class and occupation they were born into. This was difficult for some people, such as the samurai, who were warriors and so had nothing to do in a country at peace. Japan was one of the richest countries in the world in the 18th century, but it was becoming backward compared with the West, which was changing rapidly.

◁ Planting rice in a rain storm. Although farm land was scarce, Japanese peasant farmers made the most of it. By making terraces, they could grow rice on steep slopes. But they did not own the land, and the profits were made by those who collected rice as a form of tax.

## A changing country

The Tokugawa shoguns did not like change, but changes happened anyway. Thanks to better rice farming, the population grew fast. The use of money became common in trade, and a new class of merchants grew up. Because they did not produce anything, merchants were classed below the peasants. All the same, they became richer, and more powerful, than the daimyo.

### Japanese arts

*Japanese arts flourished. New, colour-printed posters, showing scenes of everyday life and people, were popular. These were a strong influence on Western art in the 19th century. In spite of government opposition, popular forms of theatre such as Kabuki and the Bunraku puppet theatre developed into true art forms in the 17th and 18th centuries. These actors (right) are dressed for the parts of a murderer and his victim in a Kabuki drama.*

## The end of the shogunate

Although the towns became rich and lively, the peasants in the countryside were still poor. Peasant rebellions broke out more often. The government of the shogun was growing weaker. In 1854, Japan was forced to open its ports to western trade. The daimyo hated the foreigners and turned against the shogun. Others realised that the powerful westerners could not be kept out.

▽ In 1853 a US naval squadron sailed into Tokyo Bay and demanded that Japan open its ports to foreign trade. The shogun unwillingly agreed. Japan's long isolation was over.

△ The Japanese believed in making ordinary things beautiful and artistic. Even tea drinking was a ceremony, held in a special room.

# The Rise of Science

*People began to understand more about nature and the universe as a result of scientific discoveries in the 17th century. The invention of instruments such as the telescope and the microscope made these advances possible. Galileo's observations proved that the Earth moves around the Sun, and Newton explained why.*

## Science in the East

Before this time, science in China, India and Islamic countries was more advanced than in Europe. The Chinese were especially good at technology. More than 1,000 years ago they invented the abacus (the first calculator), clocks, rockets, paper and printing. They knew more about medicine than people in other countries.

The Hindus in India were ahead in mathematics. They invented the idea of 0 (zero) and the numbers we use today. In Islam, the caliphs of Baghdad encouraged science, as long as it did not contradict religious teaching. Arab astronomy and geography were the best in the world. The Arabs took their mathematics from the Hindus. They translated and studied the work of ancient Greek scholars, who had been forgotten in Europe.

▷ Scholars in this 16th-century observatory in Constantinople (Istanbul) are using instruments for taking measurements of the stars. At the back are a cross-staff, a quadrant and an astrolabe, all used by travellers to work out where they were from the position of the stars. The study of the stars was important in Islam. It helped the Muslims to work out the direction of Mecca from wherever they were, so they knew in which direction to pray.

▷ When Galileo heard how a Dutchman had invented the telescope in 1608, he immediately made one himself. With it he saw that the surface of the Moon was rough and uneven.

## Sensational discoveries

1608 First telescope made by Lippershey.
1628 Harvey shows how blood circulates.
1658 Huygens makes pendulum clock.
1662 First study of statistics.
1673 Leeuwenhoek's microscope can magnify 200 times.
1676 Römer calculates speed of light.
1687 Newton publishes his theory of gravity.

## Learning about the universe

Before the 17th century, science was held back by the Christian Church, which punished anyone whose ideas disagreed with its teaching. Copernicus, a Polish monk, wrote a book on astronomy which denied the Church's belief that the Earth was the centre of the universe. He dared not publish it until he was dying, in 1543. Nearly 100 years later, an Italian called Galileo got into trouble for teaching Copernicus's ideas. He knew Copernicus was right because he had looked at the sky using a telescope. He saw that Jupiter has moons that move around it, just as our Moon moves around the Earth. Changes in the appearance of the planets showed that they were circling the Sun. Galileo's telescope solved many mysteries. He showed that the planets seem larger than the stars because they are nearer, and that the Milky Way is not just a sheet of light, but billions of separate stars.

However, Galileo could not explain why some planets move around others. It was an English scientist, Isaac Newton, who discovered the law of gravity which he explained in a book, known as Newton's *Principia* ('principles'), one of the greatest science books ever written. Newton saw that the orbit of the Moon depends on the same force that makes an apple fall to Earth – the force of gravity.

△ When Robert Hooke made his microscope he was able to see a tiny flea clearly enough to make this detailed drawing.

## Studying living things

The most sensational discoveries of the Scientific Revolution were in mathematics, physics and astronomy, but people also made important advances in other sciences, especially biology. A book on the human body by a Flemish doctor called Vesalius (1543) described the organs of the body, with brilliant drawings based on his dissections. This helped William Harvey, an Englishman, to understand how the blood circulates through the body (1628). Many discoveries followed Leeuwenhoek's invention of a better microscope. Robert Hooke, an Englishman, was the first to describe the cells of living things.

### *Scientific societies*

*Universities began to take science seriously. Gresham College, London (1575) had lectures in astronomy. Sir Isaac Newton (right) studied mathematics and science at Cambridge University, England. From 1660 scientific societies or clubs, like the English Royal Society and the French Academy of Science, were founded. By bringing scientists together to discuss their ideas, they encouraged scientific progress.*

# Louis XIV's Europe

*The powers of European kings were at their greatest in the 17th century. The French king Louis XIV was the most powerful king in Europe. Most countries were growing richer, but under the old form of royal government much of those riches were wasted.*

## Louis XIV's France

The reign of Louis XIV (1643-1715) was the longest in European history. France was a strong country with a large population, good farmland, profitable trade, and an almost unbeatable army. Louis's power had few limits; he made all important decisions himself and did not have to consult a parliament. He wanted to make France the most powerful nation in Europe by expanding her frontiers. As his soldiers invaded land belonging to other countries, European powers including the Dutch, and later the English, made alliances against France in a series of wars.

Although he won some victories in these wars, Louis did not gain much of the land he wanted. The heavy costs of war, and the deaths of men in battle, made France weaker. The king did not improve the lives of people either. The poor paid most of the taxes, and nobles and rich churchmen paid little. The population fell, farmers were paid less for their crops, and thousands of peasants died of starvation.

When Louis XIV lay dying, he told his heir, "Do not copy my love of building or my love of warfare."

▽ Louis XIV's grand and hugely expensive palace of Versailles was the wonder of Europe. Here the 'Sun King', as Louis was called, lived a life of long, boring public ceremonies. He was attended by the nobility of France, who were forced to live at court to keep them out of mischief. It was the custom that the king's subjects should be able to see him, so while Louis ate his dinner, which was cold by the time it reached him, a stream of visitors passed by to stare at him. They paid a small fee.

## The English Civil War

Like Louis XIV, Charles I (reigned 1625-49) believed God had chosen him to rule his country. But the English parliament wanted more control over how the king governed, and tried to control him by not allowing him to raise taxes. He needed Parliament's consent to do this. Charles and Parliament quarrelled and the result was civil war (1642-46). The armies of Parliament ('Roundheads') defeated the armies of the king ('Cavaliers'). When Charles plotted with his Scottish subjects to regain the throne, he was executed as a traitor to his people (above). For a few years, England was a republic, but in 1653

Oliver Cromwell, parliament's leading general, took over the government. He was called 'Lord Protector', and ruled much like a king. After Cromwell died, Charles's son was asked back to be king, and crowned Charles II in 1660.

## The European nations

In Austria, Portugal and Spain, the powers of the monarch were almost unlimited. However, Spain was no longer the greatest European power. The Spanish king Charles II (1664-1700) wanted to keep the Spanish Empire together, so he left the Spanish crown in his will to a grandson of Louis XIV. Louis's enemies did not want France to control the Spanish Empire, and in the War of the Spanish Succession (1702-14) they defeated the great French army.

The independent states in the Netherlands formed a group of republics, led by Holland. Their leader, called the stadtholder, was a monarch of a kind, but he shared power equally with the States General (parliament). In northern Europe, the Swedish Vasa kings had won an empire centred on the Baltic Sea, but Russia, under its powerful tsar, was the great and growing power in this region.

▽ Ordinary people suffered greatly in the English Civil War and in the wars in mainland Europe. Soldiers were often unpaid, and had to live on what they could steal.

# European Trading Empires

*The struggle for trade and colonies carried European wars onto other continents and brought many peoples under European control.*

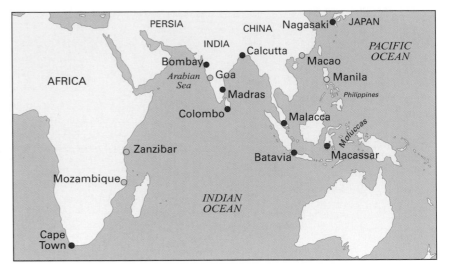

## The Dutch

The newly independent Dutch republic was a small state in the early 17th century, but it was rich and confident. Dutch wealth was based on shipping and trade. The giant Dutch merchant fleet carried most of Europe's overseas trade, and the Dutch were among the first to believe that trade was worth fighting for. They built up their trade and business empire, mainly at the expense of the Portuguese. The soldiers of the Dutch East India Company drove the Portuguese out of many trading posts in the East Indies and West Africa.

But the Dutch were soon challenged by England, a more powerful sea-going power. The English controlled the English Channel, through which the Dutch trading ships had to sail. In its attempt to break the Dutch hold on Europe's overseas trade, England fought three wars at sea between 1652 and 1674. In 1689 the Dutch prince William of Orange, became king of England, and the two rival countries united against Louis XIV's France.

**places controlled by Europeans**
- ● Dutch
- ● English
- ○ Spanish
- ○ Portuguese

## East India Companies

The trading empires of the Dutch, English, French and others were won mainly by private business companies. Merchants, or stockholders, provided the money for these companies, but they needed government support. The Dutch and English East India Companies each had a monopoly granted by its government, which meant that no other company from their country was allowed to compete with it. They were very aggressive, and used force against their foreign trading rivals. Similar companies traded in other parts of the world. In America, the Massachusetts Bay Company financed the settlement of Massachusetts in 1630. The goods that the Europeans wanted were things they could not get at home, such as silk and porcelain, tea, coffee and spices. The American colonies produced tobacco and cotton.

## Trading colonies

The Dutch East India Company founded Batavia (now Jakarta) as a rival to the Portuguese port of Malacca in 1619. It became the capital of the Dutch East Indies. The Dutch company was more powerful than any rivals in the 17th century. It captured Malacca in 1641, and secured a monopoly of trade with Japan.

In 1652 the Dutch set up a base near the Cape of Good Hope, to provide rest and supplies for ships bound for Batavia. It was a beautiful, fertile land, with few people. After 1685 the Cape attracted settlers from the Netherlands, as well as Huguenots driven out of France by Louis XIV. This was the first successful European colony in Africa.

▽ An Indian prince entertains officials of the British East India Company. Although the British became rulers of India, that was not why they went there. They wanted to make money, not run the government.

### Christian missionaries

*Besides traders, adventurers and soldiers, among the first Europeans on other continents were Roman Catholic missionaries. In Spanish America, Franciscans and Jesuits tried to protect native Americans against the greed of the conquerors, though they also helped to destroy their non-Christian customs. The greatest missionaries were Francis Xavier in Japan and Matteo Ricci, who brought Christianity to China. He tried to make Christianity fit in with Chinese customs. He was a man of great learning, who wrote books in Chinese and lived like a Chinese mandarin himself, and he was greatly respected in Beijing, where he lived (1601-10).*

*But his own Church rejected his policy of changing Christian ideas to suit Chinese traditions. The picture shows Father Ricci standing before a Christian altar with his first Chinese convert.*

## The first British Empire

The European wars of the 18th century were fought both in mainland Europe and worldwide. The main rivals, Britain and France, both wanted to increase their trade and were building overseas empires. Each of them had a strong navy to make this possible. When the Seven Years' War ended in 1763, British victories on land and sea had driven France out of Canada and India.

# The Rise of Russia

*In the 18th century a great new power appeared on the European scene: Russia. The biggest country in the world, the land ruled by the Russian tsars stretched for over 12,000 km, from the Baltic Sea to the Pacific Ocean. But much of that land was cold and barren, and its people were poor and uneducated.*

▷ The expansion of Russia. The huge Russian empire grew from the small grand duchy of Moscow, which by 1533 had thrown off Mongol rule, defeated rival princes and gained much of modern Russia.

## Northern Europe

Control of the Baltic Sea was at the centre of affairs in northern Europe. The region was rich in trade and resources. All western Europe depended on the Baltic for timber, rope, and other naval stores. Denmark grew wealthy in the 16th century from the customs duties it collected by controlling the entrance to the Baltic.

In the 17th century Sweden became the leading power. Gustavus Adolphus, the most successful general of the Thirty Years War (1618-48), made Sweden a powerful force in Europe. But the Swedes found that success produces enemies, and their power began to fail. They had some success against their enemies in the Great Northern War (1700-21), under Charles XII, but were defeated by the Russians at the Battle of Poltava (1709). The balance of power in the region was turning away from Scandinavia, in favour of larger nations on the continental mainland – Russia and Prussia.

## Russia looks west

The Grand Dukes of Moscow increased their land by conquering the Muslim territories to the east, and in 1547 Grand Duke Ivan IV took the title of tsar (emperor). Russian civilisation was strongly influenced by Byzantium, especially in religion, and the tsars saw themselves as successors to the Byzantine emperors. The defeat of Sweden in the Great Northern War extended Russia's territory to the coast of the Baltic, making Russia the greatest power in northern Europe.

Peter the Great (Peter I, reigned 1682-1725), the 'father' of modern Russia, was determined to bring his backward country up to date with western Europe. His methods were tough, sometimes cruel, but effective. He controlled troublesome groups like the boyars, who had once ruled Russia for their own selfish benefit, and replaced them with his own officials. He brought Western experts to St Petersburg as teachers, and travelled through Europe himself, picking up new ideas. He even worked in Dutch and English dockyards, disguised as 'Peter Mikhailov'.

▷ Peter built a magnificent new capital, St Petersburg, on the Baltic as his 'window on the West'. It gave Russia an important Baltic port, which put the ports of Western Europe within easy reach. Peter ordered the building of this Winter Palace, which was completed under Catherine the Great. Today it is part of a famous museum, the Hermitage.

the Russian Empire in 1533
lands gained by 1725
lands gained by 1796

## Serfs

*Most Russians were poor
peasants or serfs (right),
who were almost slaves.
They had few rights,
owned no land, never went
to school, and often died
of hunger. Desperation
often forced them into
rebellion against the
landowners. The
value of an estate
in Russia was measured not by its area but by
the number of serfs it contained. The reforms
of Peter and Catherine gave more rights to
the nobles but did not help the serfs, on whose
labour they depended.*

## Catherine the Great

Russian territory and influence continued to
grow, Catherine the Great, a German princess
who succeeded her husband, Peter III, as empress
(1762-96), dreamed of a new Russian Orthodox
Christian empire. She increased the empire through
wars against the Turks, and joined with Austria and
Prussia to divide up Poland. Like Peter, she tried to
'westernise' Russia. A rebellion of peasants and
others in 1773 made her realise that change was
needed, but her reforms only helped nobles and
townspeople, not the peasants.

▽ Although Peter tried to
make Russians look west,
towards Europe, he also
encouraged Russia's
expansion south-east,
towards the Black Sea and
Caspian Sea, and east. He
supported the Cossacks,
adventurous outlaw bands
who conquered Siberia.
He organised the
exploring expeditions
which later reached the
Pacific and Alaska.

# Europe in the 18th century

*The wars of rival royal powers in Europe continued during the 18th century. Some of the 'players' were new. Russia and Prussia now had large parts. But their ambitions were the same – to increase their power and influence.*

## The rise of Prussia

The Habsburg emperors of Austria (Holy Roman Emperors) had failed to unite Germany. At the end of the Thirty Years War (1648) Germany remained divided into many small states, with different kinds of government and different religions, Catholic and Protestant. One of these states, Brandenburg, was ruled by an able royal family, the Hohenzollens. They inherited the duchy of Prussia in eastern Germany, and in 1701 formed the kingdom of Prussia. Hardworking peasants turned the plains into a rich farming region. The Prussian nobles, the Junkers, formed a powerful military class, and the large Prussian army was the best in Europe. Protestant Prussia became a rival to Catholic Austria as the leading German power.

▽ Wolfgang Amadeus Mozart (1756-91) began performing at concerts when he was five. He was one of the great German-speaking composers who appeared in the late 18th century. Others were Haydn and Beethoven.

## Frederick the Great

With a full treasury and a large army, Frederick the Great of Prussia (Frederick II, 1740-86) was in a strong position. In 1740 he seized the rich Austrian province of Silesia. A brilliant general, he still held it after eight years of war. The struggle was renewed in the Seven Years War (1756-63), in which Austria had powerful allies – France and Russia. Prussia's only ally was Britain, which sent money but few soldiers.

Frederick was a lover of music and a friend of philosophers. He was one of a new, more modern kind of ruler in the 18th century, like Catherine the Great of Russia and the Austrian emperor Joseph II. They believed that intelligent reasoning, which had solved so many scientific problems, could also solve problems of government. They were active reformers who brought many benefits to their subjects, but, although they made some sensible changes in law, education, business affairs, and in government, they never gave up any of their royal powers.

| Main European wars 1689-1789 |
| --- |
| 1689-97 War of the 'Grand Alliance' against France |
| 1700-21 Great Northern War |
| 1702-13 War of the Spanish Succession |
| 1740-48 War of the Austrian Succession |
| 1756-63 Seven Years War |

### Coffee houses

*Coffee, imported from the Middle East, was a popular drink in Europe from the 17th century. Coffee houses in cities (right) provided a meeting place for businessmen and professional people. They could also read the new daily newspapers there. The famous insurance business, Lloyds of London, began with a group of merchants and ship-owners meeting in Lloyd's Coffee House.*

## Winners and losers

In the 18th century, France was still the greatest European power, and still the leader in style and fashion, but it no longer dominated the continent. Overseas, it lost many of its settlements and trading posts to its rival, Britain, which by 1763 ruled a large world empire. In central Europe, Habsburg Austria still seemed stronger than Prussia, but it was under threat from Russia's push towards south-east Europe. The Habsburg Empire, unlike Prussia, was made up of a mixture of people, different religions and different races (there were more Slavs than Germans). The loss of Silesia to Prussia was the first sign that Austria was in danger of losing its position as the leading power in Germany.

◁ Austrians and Prussians fight during the Seven Years War. Although Prussia suffered in the war, by 1770 it was powerful again. Besides keeping Silesia, in 1772 Frederick gained part of Poland.

▽ Craftsmanship reached a peak in 18th-century Europe. This desk was made for the king of France, the leading country in style and fashion.

## The division of Poland

While Russia and Prussia were growing, another old European nation, Poland, disappeared. The Polish monarchy was not hereditary. Polish kings were elected, which meant that other countries were always interfering to get their favourite candidate on the throne. The Polish nobles controlled the election but, like the Russian nobles, they were interested in making themselves rich, not in the good of the nation. The rest of the Poles were powerless peasants. These weaknesses allowed Poland's three powerful neighbours, Russia, Prussia and Austria, to divide the country between them. Russia took about half, the others took the rest. By 1795, Poland ceased to exist.

# The North American Colonies

*The first English colony in North America was founded in Virginia in 1607. By 1750 there were 13 British colonies lining the east coast of America. Although each colony was different, in 1776 they united to form a new nation, the United States of America.*

## The thirteen colonies

The native population in this region was small and scattered. There was space for all, and relations between colonists and Native Americans started well. The early years were hard, and many colonists died. In Massachusetts more would have died if Algonquin farmers had not helped them grow American crops. But the two groups never mixed. Thousands of Native Americans died of European diseases, and, as the colonies grew, distrust and violence increased. The peaceful Quakers of Pennsylvania treated their neighbours honourably. But some other colonists showed no respect for native rights.

There were hundreds of small nations of Native Americans. Apart from the Iroquois League, which controlled northern New York State, they seldom acted together. But in 1675, a chief called Metacom united some Massachusetts tribes and attacked colonial settlements. Although other Native Americans came to their aid, colonists attacked innocent villages in revenge.

NEW HAMPSHIRE
NEW FRANCE
NEW YORK
MASSACHUSETTS
RHODE ISLAND
CONNECTICUT
PENN-SYLVANIA
NEW JERSEY
MARYLAND
DELAWARE
NATIVE AMERICAN TERRITORY
VIRGINIA
NORTH CAROLINA
LOUISIANA
GEORGIA
SOUTH CAROLINA
FLORIDA

- █ 13 Colonies
- █ French possessions
- ☐ Spanish possessions
- — Proclamation line of 1763

△ This shows the 13 British colonies in 1756. Most people lived very close to the coast. The Proclamation line was meant to stop them moving west into Native American territory.

▷ Towns like this one in the northern colonies grew fast in the 18th century. By 1770 Philadelphia (the largest) was bigger than most European cities. Because so much of the country was wooded, most houses were built of wood.

## From Maine to Georgia

The colonies were started at different times and for different reasons. Some were business companies, hoping for profits through trade. Many of the colonists were religious refugees. The early leaders of Massachusetts were Puritans, with strict religious beliefs. The southern colonies became quite different. There, landowners were rich, thanks to crops such as tobacco and sugar, grown on large plantations worked by slaves. The colonies, especially the northern colonies later called New England, developed without much interference from England. Most had an assembly of elected representatives. There were royal governors, but the assemblies had some power because they controlled taxes.

Although most came from the British Isles, settlers also arrived from other European countries. New York was Dutch before the British took it. Germans, Swiss, Scandinavians and others settled in Pennsylvania. The British and French fought over land in Canada, and in the south.

◁ In this painting William Penn, an English Quaker leader, makes a treaty with the Delaware nation and pays for its lands (1682). His policy gave the colonists of Pennsylvania a long-lasting peace with the Native Americans.

## New foods

The animals and plants of the New World (the Americas) were different from those of the Old World. The crops from the colonies in North and South America improved the diet of Europeans with new kinds of food. Potatoes were the most important, then maize (sweet corn). Tomatoes, green peppers and turkeys were welcome luxuries.

## Trade and industry

Britain expected its colonies to provide cheap raw materials for British industries, and then to buy British goods. They were not expected to have their own industries, or to trade with other countries. The southern colonies supplied crops that needed a warm climate, such as tobacco, rice and sugar (a big crop in the West Indies). The northern colonies had poorer soil and a colder climate, but supplied fish and furs. They also developed industries of their own, such as shipbuilding. They even found ways to trade with other countries.

### Harvard University

*The first successful university was founded in 1636 in Cambridge, Massachusetts. The town was named after Cambridge, England, where many Puritan ministers had trained. The university was named after one of these ministers, John Harvard, who left his money and library to the university.*

# The Slave Trade

*European traders found few spices and little gold when they first arrived in West Africa. But they soon discovered another, very valuable product – people. Between the 17th and 19th centuries about 20 million people were captured in Africa, carried across the Atlantic, and sold as slaves to colonists in the Americas.*

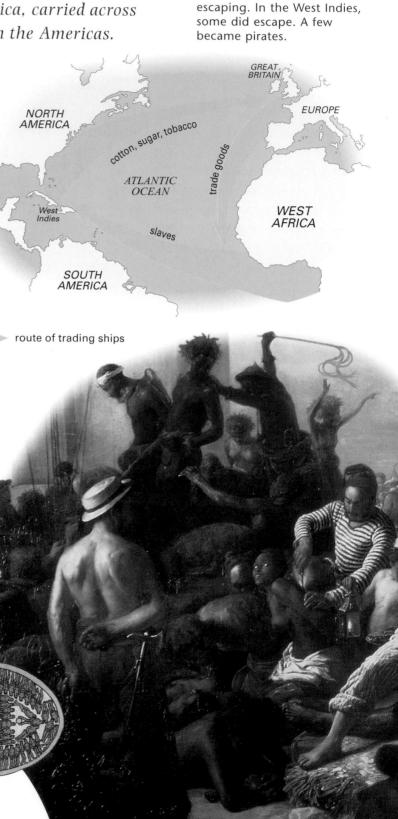

▽ The 'triangular' trade. Sometimes the prisoners on a slave ship rebelled. But they had almost no chance of escaping. In the West Indies, some did escape. A few became pirates.

## Cheap labour

The first African slaves were sold in Portugal as early as 1434, and by 1700 the slave trade was a big international business. European colonists in the Caribbean and other warm regions in the New World needed large numbers of workers for their sugar and cotton plantations. They paid high prices for African slaves, who were good workers – and did not have to be paid.

GREAT BRITAIN
NORTH AMERICA
EUROPE
cotton, sugar, tobacco
trade goods
ATLANTIC OCEAN
West Indies
WEST AFRICA
slaves
SOUTH AMERICA

→ route of trading ships

## Slavery

Slavery has existed in most countries since ancient times. Trade in slaves, run mainly by Muslims, existed in East and other parts of Africa too, but the slave trade to the Americas was particularly cruel. People were uprooted and shipped like cattle to another continent, with no hope of freedom. Families were broken up, and slaves were often overworked and cruelly treated on the plantations. Many owners thought blacks were not fully human, which made slavery seem less evil. In West Africa, large regions were ruined by the raids of slavers from the coast.

STORE ROOM
STORE ROOM

△ A diagram showing how a slave ship was filled with its 'cargo'. Not an inch was wasted.

## The triangular trade

Huge profits could be made in the slave trade. The ships started out from European Atlantic ports, such as Liverpool in England or Bordeaux in France, carrying cheap guns, strong drink and other goods. They sold these to people on the West African coast, who used the guns to round up helpless villagers from farther inland. The captives were sold to the European traders, and shipped across the Atlantic to be sold again, at a large profit, at auctions in the colonies. The ships then took on cargoes of sugar or other produce from the colonies, which they carried back to Europe. With luck, they made a profit on all three parts of this 'triangular' trade.

### Toussaint l'Ouverture

*In 1791 the slaves in Haiti, led by Toussaint l'Ouverture (right), rebelled against their vicious French masters. The French promised to end slavery, and Toussaint, now governor, fought for the French against Spanish and British invaders. Later the French sent an army to restore French rule. They captured Toussaint, who died in France, but the French were defeated and Haiti became independent in 1804.*

## The abolition of slavery

As time went by, more and more Europeans were disgusted by slavery and the cruelties of the slave trade. Britain, the chief trading nation, made the trade illegal in 1807. But there was still a big demand for slaves in the plantations of the American South, the West Indies and Brazil, so the trade went on. Slavery continued in the Southern states until the Civil War (1861-65), and in Brazil until 1888. In some countries slavery was still legal up to the 1960s.

◁ Slaves, dealers and European traders on a slave ship off West Africa. A woman is being branded with an owner's mark.

# The Early Modern World

*In this period, all the different parts of the world came into contact for the first time. But people were not drawn together more closely. They were divided by different ideas and customs, and especially by different religions. The*

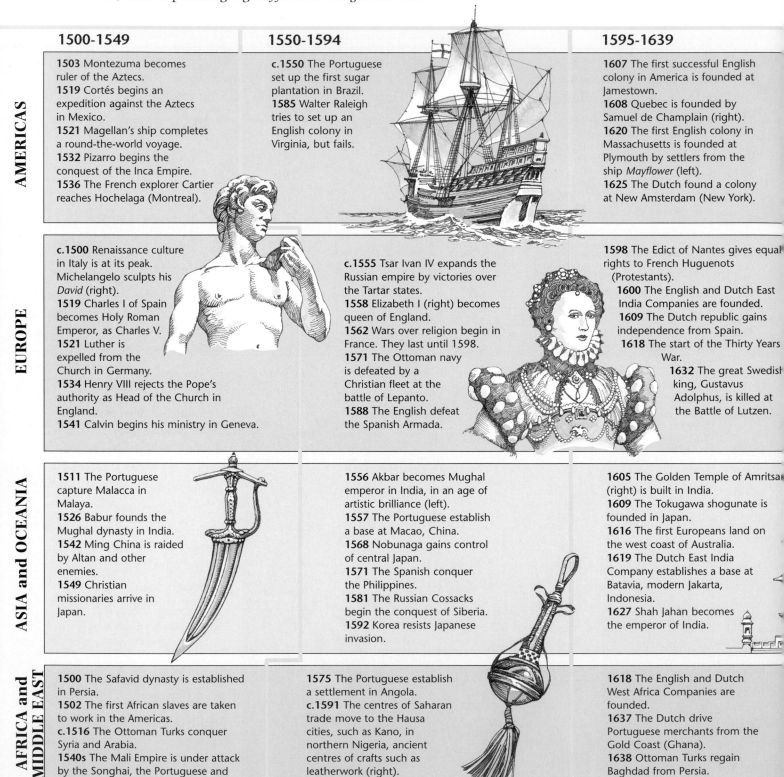

## AMERICAS

### 1500-1549

**1503** Montezuma becomes ruler of the Aztecs.
**1519** Cortés begins an expedition against the Aztecs in Mexico.
**1521** Magellan's ship completes a round-the-world voyage.
**1532** Pizarro begins the conquest of the Inca Empire.
**1536** The French explorer Cartier reaches Hochelaga (Montreal).

### 1550-1594

**c.1550** The Portuguese set up the first sugar plantation in Brazil.
**1585** Walter Raleigh tries to set up an English colony in Virginia, but fails.

### 1595-1639

**1607** The first successful English colony in America is founded at Jamestown.
**1608** Quebec is founded by Samuel de Champlain (right).
**1620** The first English colony in Massachusetts is founded at Plymouth by settlers from the ship *Mayflower* (left).
**1625** The Dutch found a colony at New Amsterdam (New York).

## EUROPE

**c.1500** Renaissance culture in Italy is at its peak. Michelangelo sculpts his *David* (right).
**1519** Charles I of Spain becomes Holy Roman Emperor, as Charles V.
**1521** Luther is expelled from the Church in Germany.
**1534** Henry VIII rejects the Pope's authority as Head of the Church in England.
**1541** Calvin begins his ministry in Geneva.

**c.1555** Tsar Ivan IV expands the Russian empire by victories over the Tartar states.
**1558** Elizabeth I (right) becomes queen of England.
**1562** Wars over religion begin in France. They last until 1598.
**1571** The Ottoman navy is defeated by a Christian fleet at the battle of Lepanto.
**1588** The English defeat the Spanish Armada.

**1598** The Edict of Nantes gives equal rights to French Huguenots (Protestants).
**1600** The English and Dutch East India Companies are founded.
**1609** The Dutch republic gains independence from Spain.
**1618** The start of the Thirty Years War.
**1632** The great Swedish king, Gustavus Adolphus, is killed at the Battle of Lutzen.

## ASIA and OCEANIA

**1511** The Portuguese capture Malacca in Malaya.
**1526** Babur founds the Mughal dynasty in India.
**1542** Ming China is raided by Altan and other enemies.
**1549** Christian missionaries arrive in Japan.

**1556** Akbar becomes Mughal emperor in India, in an age of artistic brilliance (left).
**1557** The Portuguese establish a base at Macao, China.
**1568** Nobunaga gains control of central Japan.
**1571** The Spanish conquer the Philippines.
**1581** The Russian Cossacks begin the conquest of Siberia.
**1592** Korea resists Japanese invasion.

**1605** The Golden Temple of Amritsar (right) is built in India.
**1609** The Tokugawa shogunate is founded in Japan.
**1616** The first Europeans land on the west coast of Australia.
**1619** The Dutch East India Company establishes a base at Batavia, modern Jakarta, Indonesia.
**1627** Shah Jahan becomes the emperor of India.

## AFRICA and MIDDLE EAST

**1500** The Safavid dynasty is established in Persia.
**1502** The first African slaves are taken to work in the Americas.
**c.1516** The Ottoman Turks conquer Syria and Arabia.
**1540s** The Mali Empire is under attack by the Songhai, the Portuguese and the Moroccans.

**1575** The Portuguese establish a settlement in Angola.
**c.1591** The centres of Saharan trade move to the Hausa cities, such as Kano, in northern Nigeria, ancient centres of crafts such as leatherwork (right).

**1618** The English and Dutch West Africa Companies are founded.
**1637** The Dutch drive Portuguese merchants from the Gold Coast (Ghana).
**1638** Ottoman Turks regain Baghdad from Persia.

*aggressive behaviour of Europeans, whose ships and armies travelled all over the world, caused serious disturbances in other continents, especially in the Americas. It had less effect, at first, on the great empires of Asia.*

## 1640-1684

**1654** The Dutch are driven from Brazil.
**1664** The English obtain New York from the Dutch.
**1684** La Salle sails down the Mississippi and claims the region, called Louisiana, for France.

**1642** Civil war breaks out in England, between the king, Charles I, and parliament.
**1649** King Charles I of England is executed.
**1654** Russia gains control of the Ukraine.
**1658** The peace of Roskilde between Sweden and Denmark marks the high point of the Swedish Empire.
**1683** The Ottoman Turks besiege Vienna.

**1644** The Qing (Manchu) dynasty is founded in China.
**1645** Tasman reaches New Zealand.
**c.1653** The Taj Mahal is built at Agra in India.
**1661** Millions die in India after two years of drought.

**c.1650** The slave trade begins to spread inland from the coastal regions of West Africa.
**1652** Cape Colony is founded by the Dutch East India Company, as a base for supplying their trade with the East Indies.

## 1685-1729

**1713** European settlers drive the Tuscarora and other Native Americans from the Carolinas.
**1726** Nathaniel Bacon leads a rebellion against the governor of British Virginia, in an effort to drive Native Americans out of the colony.

**1699** The Habsburgs regain Hungary from the Ottoman Turks.
**1700** The Great Northern War breaks out, between Sweden and its neighbours, including Russia.
**1703** St Petersburg is founded as the new Russian capital.
**1704** Blenheim Palace (left) is the queen's reward to the British Duke of Marlborough for his victory against France, in the War of the Spanish Succession.
**1707** England and Scotland are united by the Act of Union.

**1690** Calcutta is founded by the British in Bengal, India.
**c.1695** China establishes control over Mongolia.
**c.1700** The Hindu Mahratta state in India revives under its peshwas (hereditary chief ministers).
**1720** China gains control of Tibet.

**c.1690** Asante power, rich in gold (this eagle, left, is an example), rises in West Africa.
**c.1700** The Oyo kingdom of the Yoruba is the dominant state in the region of Nigeria.
**c.1700** Lunda states form an empire including southern Congo and much of Angola and Zambia.
**1705** Algerian tribes reject Ottoman rule and win independence under the Dey of Algiers.

## 1730-1774

**1741** Ships from a Russian expedition led by Vitus Bering, a Dane, sail from Siberia across the Bering Strait to Alaska.
**1759** The British take Quebec and conquer New France (French Canada).
**c.1770** The Iroquois League of Native American peoples begins to break up. The Iroquois made this shoe (right).

**1740** Prussia seizes Silesia in the War of the Austrian Succession.
**1751** The first volumes of Diderot's *Encyclopedia* are published in France.
**1756** The Seven Years War begins, with Prussia and Britain against Austria, France, Russia and others.
**c.1769** James Watt invents a better steam engine.
**1774** The treaty of Kuchuk Kainarji leads to growing Russian influence in the European provinces of the Ottoman Empire.

**1736** Qianlong (left) becomes emperor of China.
**c.1750** The Chinese empire expands to include Tibet.
**1757** Alaungpaya re-establishes the kingdom of Myanmar.
**1757** Victory at Plassey in north-east India leads to British control of Bengal.
**1771** The British Captain Cook explores the coast of New South Wales.

**1736** Nadir Shah destroys the Safavid dynasty in Persia.
**1747** Afghan chiefs elect Ahmed Shah Durani as king of Afghanistan and he creates a powerful state.

# Who's Who

**Abbas the Great** (1558-1629), shah of Persia from 1586. The greatest of the Safavid rulers, he created a professional army and greatly increased Persian territory, driving out the Uzbeks and winning land from the Ottoman Turks. He encouraged the arts and trade, granting rights to Dutch and English merchants.

**Akbar the Great** (1542-1605), Mughal emperor of India from 1556. After conquering most of India, he set out to make it a strong and united empire, in which Muslims and Hindus were equal. He even tried to introduce a new religion that combined Hindu and Muslim beliefs.

**Champlain, Samuel de** (1567-1635), French explorer. His journeys in Canada took him up the St Lawrence River to Lake Huron, and south to Cape Cod. He saw Canada as a place for settlement, not just making money from furs. He founded Quebec in 1608 and encouraged settlers in 'New France'.

**Columbus, Christopher** (?1451-1506), navigator, born in Genoa, Italy. Hired by Spain to find a sea route to the Far East in 1492, he reached the West Indies. In three more voyages, he explored Caribbean islands and the South American coast. In 1500 he was arrested. He died poor and neglected.

**Cromwell, Oliver** (1599-1658), English army general and ruler. A country squire and member of parliament, he became the most successful general on parliament's side in the English Civil War. When quarrels between different groups made republican government impossible, Cromwell became ruler as 'Lord Protector' (1653-58).

**Erasmus** (Geert Geerts, 1466-1536), Dutch scholar. He was a leader of the Renaissance in northern Europe and a friend of many European scholars. Like Luther, he wanted reforms in the Church, but he opposed the founding of new, Protestant Churches.

**Frederick the Great** (1712-86), king of Prussia from 1740. The best general of his time, his wars increased Prussian territory and its standing in Europe, while his government reforms strengthened the kingdom. He was also a good musician, a friend of French philosophers, and the author of many books on history.

**Galileo Galilei** (1564-1642), Italian scientist. The greatest scientist of his time, he was born in Pisa and used its leaning tower to prove that light and heavy objects fall at the same speed. He discovered the principle of the pendulum, and made a telescope to study the Moon. His ideas angered the Church which tried to stop his studies.

**Ivan IV** (1530-84), tsar of Russia from 1533. He strengthened royal government, fought many wars to increase his lands, and supported the Cossack conquest of Siberia. After 1560 he became savage, slaughtering the wealthy boyars, killing his son in a rage, so earning his nickname, 'The Terrible'.

**Kangxi** (1654-1722), emperor of China from 1661. He strengthened the Qing (Manchu) dynasty, crushing rebellion in the south and defeating the last Ming forces, and gained control of Tibet. He encouraged scholars and artists, and accepted Christian missionaries for their knowledge of science.

**Leonardo da Vinci** (1452-1519), Italian artist, engineer and scientist. A great genius of the Renaissance, he worked mainly for the rulers of Florence, Milan and France, designing weapons, machines and buildings, as well as painting. His portrait of a lady, known as the *Mona Lisa*, is perhaps the world's most famous painting.

**Louis XIV** (1638-1715), king of France from 1643, the longest reign in European history. He took over the government after the death of his first minister Cardinal Mazarin in 1661. Powerful and ambitious, he dominated European affairs, but while his court was hugely rich, poor people became poorer, and the last of his wars ended in defeat.

**Luther, Martin** (1483-1546), priest and teacher. He began the Reformation in Germany. He was condemned by the Pope and the Holy Roman Emperor, but protected by the ruler of Saxony. In the 1520s he organised the German Protestant Church.

**Newton, Sir Isaac** (1642-1727), English mathematician. The outstanding genius of the 'scientific revolution', he explained how the universe works according to the law of gravity. Among many discoveries, he showed that white light is made up of rays that make different colours when passed through a prism.

**Peter the Great** (1672-1725), tsar of Russia from 1682. Determined, energetic, ruthless, Peter set out to modernise Russia and make it a great power by copying more advanced countries like France. His reforms covered education, religion and every part of government, and his wars increased Russian territory to the east and west.

**Philip II** (1527-98), king of Spain from 1556. He also ruled much of Italy, the Netherlands, and the Spanish Empire in America. Hardworking and honest, he was a keen defender of Roman Catholicism. But he failed to end the Dutch revolt, his Armada against England was a disaster, and his policies weakened Spain.

**Richelieu, Cardinal** (1585-1642), French statesman. As first minister of Louis XIII, he directed the government for 20 years, increasing royal power and weakening the Protestant Huguenots. But in the Thirty Years War he sided with the Protestant states against the Habsburgs and made France the strongest power in Europe.

**Shakespeare, William** (1564-1616), English playwright and poet. He acted and wrote for a company that owned the Globe Theatre, in London. He wrote about 36 plays including tragedies (like *Hamlet*), and comedies (like *Twelth Night*) which are still performed all over the world.

**Suleiman the Magnificent** (reigned 1520-66), Ottoman Turkish sultan. The Ottoman Empire was at its greatest in his reign. He won new lands in the Middle East, Europe and North Africa, gaining the whole Arab world. At home, he built splendid buildings, reformed the law and made taxes more fair.

# Glossary

**absolute ruler**  A king or other ruler whose power is not limited by laws.

**allies**  Countries, or other groups, who join together for some cause, especially in war.

**artillery**  Large guns firing cannon balls or, in later times, explosives.

**Asia Minor**  The region of Asia nearest to Europe, roughly the same as modern Turkey.

**boyars**  The old class of Russian nobles, from about the 11th century.

**calligraphy**  Beautiful handwriting. It was one of the chief forms of art in ancient Egypt, in the monasteries of Europe, and in China and Japan.

**caravan**  A group of traders, and sometimes other people, travelling in a group for safety. Traders in desert regions always travelled in caravans.

**civilisation**  A group of people who have reached a state of development that includes living in cities, organised government, a written language, fine arts and learning.

**colony**  A settlement of people in another country, or a country that is ruled by another one.

**Cossacks**  Meaning 'adventurers', bands of people, mainly in Russia, who lived in their own groups almost independent of the government.

**democracy**  A country or form of government where power depends on the votes of the people.

**dissenters**  People who disagree with accepted laws or beliefs, especially in religion.

**dynasty**  A ruling family, where the title is passed down from each ruler to his or her heir.

**economy**  The management of the whole wealth of a state (or another type of community), including money, trade, and industry.

**empire**  A state which also controls other peoples or states.

**finance**  The management of all money matters.

**galley**  A type of ship driven mainly by oars, though some also had sails.

**hereditary title**  A title that is passed down in one family, from its holder to his or her heir.

**heresy**  A religious belief that opposes the accepted beliefs of the time.

**Huguenots**  French Protestants in the 16th and 17th centuries.

**immigrants**  People who have settled in a foreign country, often because of persecution in their own country.

**irrigation**  Watering of fields by the use of canals or channels.

**janissary**  A professional soldier of the Ottoman Empire.

**Latin America**  The countries of Mexico and Central and South America, where Spanish or Portuguese are spoken.

**legend**  A story that is probably based on true events.

**mercenary**  A professional soldier, willing to fight for anyone who pays him.

**merchant**  A person who lives by buying and selling goods. It usually means someone quite rich, more than a simple trader.

**Middle Ages**  The period in Europe between the end of the Roman Empire and the Renaissance of the 15th century.

**Middle East**  The region of south-west Asia from the Mediterranean to Afghanistan.

**militia**  An armed force. Unlike an army, a militia is a local group of part-time soldiers, who are called up in an emergency, such as a rebellion.

**missionary**  Someone, usually a Christian, who teaches their religion to people of other beliefs.

**monastery**  A community of people (monks) who live according to strict religious rules.

**mutiny**  A rebellion by soldiers or sailors.

**Near East**  The region around the eastern Mediterranean, sometimes including Egypt and south-east Europe.

**parliament**  A government assembly, made up of people elected by the citizens. In modern democratic countries, parliament is often the body that makes the laws.

**patriotism**  A person's love of his or her country.

**plantation**  A large farm or estate, usually in a warm country, that grows one main crop, often for export, and has its own workers.

**pope**  The head of the Roman Catholic Church.

**porcelain**  A very fine, hard type of pottery, which light will shine through. It was made in China 1,200 years ago, but in Europe only since the 18th century.

**proclamation**  An official announcement.

**Protestants**  People who, during the European Reformation, 'protested' against the Roman Catholic Church and formed their own Churches.

**Puritans**  Protestants in the 16th and 17th centuries who wanted a simpler, stricter form of religion.

**regime**  A government. It may mean any kind of government, but is often used for a military government or dictatorship.

**renaissance**  Meaning 'rebirth', a time of lively developments in the arts and learning, especially in Europe in the 15th and 16th centuries.

**samurai**  A Japanese warrior who belonged to a class like the knights in Europe and followed a strict code of honour and duty.

**seal**  An instrument with a raised design for making a pattern in, for example, a clay tablet.

**serf**  A person in the service of a lord, who 'owns' him or her. Serfs were not quite slaves, as they had some rights.

**shogun**  The military governor, or ruler, of Japan from the 12th to 19th centuries.

**shrine**  A holy place or building, such as the tomb of a saint, which pilgrims visit.

**siege**  An attack on a castle or town defended by stone walls.

**statesman**  A politician or government official of great ability, especially one who has an influence on international affairs.

**suffrage**  The right to vote.

**sultan**  A Muslim ruler, especially the ruler of the Ottoman Turkish empire.

**vizier**  An important minister in some Muslim countries. The chief minister of the Ottoman empire was called the grand vizier.

# Index

# Index

# Index

# Acknowledgements

Picture research by Caroline Wood

The publisher would like to thank the following for illustrations:

Gerry Ball; p11b
Chris Brown; p10-11t, p13t, p26-27, p31b, p36
Tim Clarey; p29, p30t, p44
Gino D'Achille; back cover, p19b, p20b, 35t, 35b, p42-43
Barbara Lofthouse; p12t, p16t
Steve Noon; p24b, p85t, p28b, p38b
Olive Pearson; all maps
Robbie Polley; p39br
Martin Sanders; p9t, p20t

The publisher would like to thank the following for permission to use photographs:

Front Cover BAL; p8 Museum of The Royal Pharmaceutical Society of Great Britain; p9br ET; p10bl MH; p11bl The Royal Collection Her Majesty Queen Elizabeth II; p11tr BAL, "Private Collection, The Stapleton Collection"; p12b BAL, "Bibliothèque de Protestantisme,France"; p13r ET, Museum of Fine Arts Lausanne; p14b ET, Private Collection; p15t ET, "The Archaeological Museum of Lima, Peru"; p15bl Mary Evans Picture Library; p16cl BAL, "Thyssen-Bornemisza Collection, Madrid, Spain"; p16br National Trust Photographic Library, Matthew Antrobus; p17t AKG; p18 BAL, "Museo Correr, Venice,Italy"; p19tr BAL, "Louvre,Paris,France"; p21t ET, British Library Add 7880; p21r Sonia Halliday Photographs; p22tr BAL, "V&A, London, UK"; p22bl BAL, "V&A, London,UK"; p23b Magnum, George Rodger; p24c "Ashmolean Museum, Oxford", ; p25b Magnum, Marc Riboud; p26bl ET, "Oriental Art Museum, Genoa"; p27tr MH, "V&A,London"; p27br ET, British Museum; p28t ET; p29c Science & Society Picture Library, Science Museum; p30b BAL, "Chateau de Versailles, France,Giraudon"; p31tr Execution of Charles I by an unknown artist reproduced by permission of The Earl of Rosebery (on loan to the Scottish National Portrait Gallery); p32-33 Photo MH, V&A; p33r ET; p34-35 Robert Harding, E.Rooney; p36-37 AKG, "Heeresgeschichtliches Museum,Vienna(detail)"; p37t AKG, Cameraphoto; p37b BAL, "Chateau de Versailles, France"; p39t "Abby Aldrich Rockefeller Folk Art Center, Williamsburg, VA"; p40-41 BAL, "Wilberforce House Museum, Hull, Humberside, UK"; p41tr BAL, "Bibliothèque Nationale, Giraudon";

Key: BAL = Bridgeman Art Library; BM = The British Museum; V&A = Victoria & Albert Museum; ET = E.T. Archive; SPL = Science Photo Library;
   AKG = AKG London; MH = Michael Holford